Python

Python Programming: Learn Python Programming In A Day - A Comprehensive Introduction To The Basics Of Python & Computer Programming

Steve Gold

Table of Contents

Chapter Three

Chapter Five

Functions

Function Parameters

Local Variables

The Global Statement

Default Argument Values

Keyword Arguments

Varargs Parameters

The Return Statement

Docstrings

Chapter Six

Modules

Introduction

The open-source, high-level programming language, Python, which was developed by Guido van Possum back in the late 80's uses an easy-to-learn yet concise syntax which is perfect for those who are aiming to develop complex code in as short a time as possible.

While the idea of learning Python programming may at first seem like a daunting task, with the right guidance you'll be up and running in no time, whether you're new to Python or new to programming entirely! In this wonderfully easy to follow guide, we've stripper away the filler to make things as simple as possible for the beginner to take their first steps into the world of Python. The information is presented clearly, in an easy-to-follow, step-by-step manner with the aim of minimizing the chances of confusion, while providing the reader with all of the essential information they'll require.

Are you ready to take your first steps towards mastering Python? Let's get started!

Chapter One

Preparing Your Programming Environment

When it comes to installing Python, you might not have to if you have a version of Linux installed on your computer. If you'd like to check to see if you have python installed, you can open your start menu and type 'python' into the search box. If nothing comes up, then you need to install it.

There are a few different operating systems out there, so let's go over how to install Python on each one of them.

Installing Python on Windows

You can visit https://www.python.org/downloads/ in order to download the most recent version of Python. The installation is just like any other Windows software. Just be sure you check the option Add Python 3.5 to PATH while installing.

To change your install location, click on the Customize installation option and click Next. Then enter C:\python35 as the install location.

If it's not checked, then check the Add Python to environment variables.

You can select to install the Launcher for every user on the computer or not, it doesn't really matter, unless someone else plans on using the language, too. Launcher will be utilized to shift between diverse versions of Python that's installed, too.

If your path wasn't set right, then follow these steps in order to fix it. Otherwise, you go on to Running Python Prompt on Windows.

DOS Prompt

If you'd like to use Python from the Windows command line or the DOS prompt, then you have to set the PATH variable correctly.

For Windows 2000, 2003, and XP, click on the Control Panel, go to System, click on Advanced, and then go into Environment Variables. Then click on the variable name PATH. Select Edit and add C:\Python35 to the end of what is already currently there. Of course, use the right directory name.

For Windows Vista, click the Start button and choose the Control Panel. Click System and you will see a section that talks about viewing basic information about the computer and on the left you will see a list of tasks, the last of which will be Advanced system settings. Click on that.

The Advanced tab will be shown, so click on Environment Variables on the bottom right. In the lower box, that's titled System Variables, scroll down to Path and click on the Edit button. Change your path appropriately.

Restart the computer.

For Windows 7 and 8, you have to right click on the Computer from the desktop and select Properties or click Start and choose the Control Panel – System and

Security – System. Click on the Advanced system settings on your left and click on the Advanced button. Click on Environment Variables at the bottom and under the System variables, you have to look for the PATH variable. Then select and press Edit.

Go to the end of the line and put in the appropriate folder name.

Click OK and you're finished!

Running Python Prompt on Windows

For those who are using Windows, you can run your interpreter in the command line if you've set the PATH variable right. To open the terminal, click the start button and then just click Run. In the dialog box, type in cmd and press the enter key.

Then, type python and ensure there aren't any errors.

Installing Python on Mac OS X

For those who are running Mac OS X, you'll want to use Homebrew, and install python 3. To verify, open your terminal by pressing Command+Space to open the Spotlight search. Type in Terminal and press the enter key. Now, run python 3 and ensure there are not any errors.

Installation on Linux

For those who are using Linux, use your distribution package manager in order to install Python 3. For example, Debian and Ubuntu users should put *sudo apt-get update && sudo apt-get install python 3* in their terminal.

To verify, open it up by pressing Alt and F2 and entering gnome-terminal. If it doesn't work, then refer back to the documentation for the Linux type you have. Run to make sure there are not any errors.

Installing the Python Text Editor

You can't type all your text into the command prompt to run a program because you'd have to do it every time. You need a compiler that's going to read Python for you and you'll need a text editor, but using Notepad on Windows is a very bad idea. It's going to get messy and sometimes it just doesn't work.

There are three editors that are recommended. These are:

PyCharm

Vim

Emacs

You can go to their respective websites and follow their instructions for downloading them. Once you have them open, you can begin your first program!

Your First Program

You might be thinking, uh oh, not again, but the Hello World program is the first program that every programmer learns to run because it teaches you the very basics of programming in any language. Besides, for those who are doing this for the first time in any language, it's pretty exciting!

Open your editor and open up a new file and call it hello.py. Type in this:

```
print("hello world")
```

Save the file where you now you're going to remember it and be sure it's in its own folder with your programs.

To run the program:

Open the terminal window.

Change directory to where you saved your file.

Run the program by entering the command hello.py in your command line. The output will be a box that says 'hello world' in it!

Python programs are made up of statements. In your first program, you have only one statement. In this statement, you call the print *statement* to which you supply the text 'hello world.'

In the next chapter, we're going to take a look at the basics of a python program!

Chapter Two

The Basics

If just displaying hello world isn't enough for you, and you want more, then you can do this with python. If you want to take an input, manipulate that input, and get something out of it, then you're looking at the right programming language. You can do this with python constants and variables, and you'll learn a few more concepts in this chapter.

Comments

Comments are any text that is the right of the pound symbol they're mainly used as notes for the person who's reading the program. For example:

```
print('hello world') #Take note that print is a function
```

You should add useful comments in order to explain assumptions, important details, important decisions, problems you're attempting to solve, and problems you're attempting to overcome in the program.

This is useful for the person reading the program so they're easily able to understand what the program is attempting to accomplish. Remember, this person could be you after six months of working on a program!

Literal Constants

An example would be a number such as six, 1.46, or a string such as *'This is a string'*. They are called literal because the value of the constant is literal. The number two will always represent itself and not anything else. It's a constant because the value is not able to be changed. Therefore, all these are referred to as literal constants.

Strings

Strings are sequences of characters. They are basically just words. You'll be using them in almost every Python program you write, so you need to pay attention to this section.

Single Quote

You can specify a string using a single quote such as 'I love chocolate.' All white spaces and tabs in the quote are preserved as they are.

Double Quote

Strings in the double quotes work exactly the same way a string does in a single quote. An example would be "What is your gender?"

Triple Quotes

You can specify a multi-line string using a triple quote, which are """" or "". You can use a single quote and a double quote freely in the triple quotes. For example:

"'This is a string that has many lines. This is the first one.

This is the second one.

"What's your favorite color?," I asked.

He said "Blue."

"'

An important note to make is that strings are immutable. This means that once you've made it, you can't change it. While this might seem like it's a terrible thing, it's actually not. You'll see why this isn't a limitation in many programs later on in the book.

Format Method

Sometimes, you might want to make strings from different information. This is where the format () method is going to be useful.

Save these lines as a file name str_format.py:

birthdate = 1986

name = 'Jeffery'

print('{0} was born in {1}'.format(name, birthdate))

print('Why does {0} play the guitar?'.format(name))

Output:

$ python str_format.py

Jeffery was born in 1986

Why does Jeffery play the guitar?

Strings are used for certain specifications, and the format method is able to be used to swap in those stipulations with the matching arguments to that format method.

Observe the first usage where {0} corresponds to the variable 'name' which is the first argument to the format method. In addition, the second specification is {1}, which corresponds to the variable 'birthdate' which is the second argument to the format method. Note that Python begins counting from zero, which means the first position is at index 0, the second is at index 1, and so on and so forth.

Escape Sequences

Suppose you'd like to have a string that has a single quote ('), how will you specify that string? For example, the string "What's your gender?". You can't specify 'What's your gender?' because python is then confused as to where the string begins and ends. So you have to specify that this single quote doesn't indicate the end of the string. This is able to be done with the help of what's known as an *escape sequence.* You identify the single quote as \'. Take note of the backslash. You can identify your string as 'What\'s your gender?'.

Another way you can specify this string is "What's your gender?" with the double quotes. You have to use the escape sequence for using a double quote in a double quoted string. You also have to indicate the backslash using the escape sequence\\.

So what if you'd like to specify a two-line string? You can do this with a triple-quoted string, or you can use an escape sequence for the new line's character - \n to indicate the beginning of the new line. An example would be:

'here is your first line \nAnd here is your second line'

Another useful one is to know is the tab: \t. There are many others out there, so be sure you make yourself familiar with them.

One thing you should take note of in a string is a single backlash at the end of the line means that the string is continuing on the next line, but no new line has been added. For example:

"Here is your first sentence. \

Here is your second sentence."

Will look like:

"Here is your first sentence. Here is your second sentence."

Raw String

If you have to specify some strings where there is no special processing such as an escape sequence, then what you have to do is specify a raw string by prefixing an r or R to it. An example would be:

R"A new line is indicated by \n"

Variables

Using the literal constants is a little boring, and you need a way to store any information and manipulate it, too. That's where variables come in. These are exactly what the name implies. Their value varies, and you can store anything using them. These are just parts of the computer's memory where you store information. Unlike a literal constant, you need a method of accessing these and hence you give them names.

Identifier Naming

Variables are an example of an identifier. These are names that are given to identify something. There are a few rules you need to follow for naming them.

The first character has to be a letter of the alphabet or an underscore.

The remainder of the name can consist of underscores, letters, or digits.

The names are case-sensitive.

An example of a valid identifier name is *name_3_4,* an example of an invalid one is *9_5_a.*

Data Types

Variables are able to hold values of varying types known as data types. The basic types are strings and numbers that you've already learned about. In a later chapter, you'll see how you can make your own types using classes.

Object

Remember that Python refers to anything that's used in a program as an object. Rather than saying 'the something' you say 'the object.'

How to Write Python Programs

So for PyCharm, to write a Python Program, you just open up PyCharm, create a new file with the filename that was mentioned, type the program code that was given in the example, right click, and then run the current file.

It's that easy!

For another editor, open the editor of choice, type the program code that was given, save it as a file with the filename mentioned in the example, run the interpreter with the command python program.py to run the program.

Logical And Physical Line

A physical line is what you see when you write your program. The logical line is what the program is seeing as a single statement. The program automatically assumes that every physical line is corresponding to a logical line.

An example of a logical one would be a statement like 'hello world'. If this were a line by itself, then this corresponds to a physical line.

The language encourages the use of a single statement for every line which makes your code more readable.

If you'd like to specify more than a single logical line on a single physical line, then you have to use the semicolon, which will indicate the end of a logical line or statement.

Indentation

Whitespace is actually important in this programming language. Actually, the whitespace at the beginning of a line is very important. This is known as an indentation. Spaces and tabs at the beginning or your logical line are used to determine the indentation level of your logical line, which is then used to determine the grouping of statements.

This means that the statements that go together have to have the same indentation level. Every such set of statements is known as a block.

To indent, use four spaces. This is the official recommendation of the programming language. Good editors automatically do this for you. Be sure you use a consistent number of indentations, otherwise, the program doesn't run or will have some unexpected behaviors.

Now that you know about comments, constants, strings, variables, objects, and how to write the program let's look at operators and expressions.

Chapter Three

Operators and Expressions

Most logical lines or statements you write are going to have expressions. A simple example would be 1+1. An expression is able to be broken down into an operator and an operand.

Operators are the functionality that does something and are represented by symbols like + or by special keywords. They require a little data to operate on, and this data is known as the operand. In this case, 1 and 1 are the operands.

Operators

We're going to briefly take a look at the operators and their uses. Note that you can evaluate an expression that's given in the examples by using the interpreter. For example, to test the expression 1+1, use the interactive interpreter prompt:

```
>>>1+1

2

>>>4*1

4

>>>
```

Let's look at a quick overview of some of the available operators.

+ (plus): this adds to objects together, such as 1+1 which equates to 2.

- (minus): this subtracts two objects, such as 1-1 which equates to 0.

* (multiply): this multiplies two numbers together or returns the string repeated that many times, such as 3*3 equals 9. 'la' * 4 equals 'lalalala'.

** (power) this returns x to the power of y, such as 4**4 equals 256. It's the same as 4*4*4*4.

/ (divide): this divides two objects, such as 12/4 which equates to 3.

// (divide and floor): this means x is divided by y and rounds the answer down to the nearest whole number, such as 17 // 4 is 4.

% (modulo): this returns the remainder of a division, such as 14 % 4 is 2.

<< (left shift): this shifts bits of the number to the left by the number of bits you specify. For example, 2 << 2 equates to 8.

>> (right shift): shifts the bits of the number to the right by the number of bits that's been specified, so 11>> 1 is five.

These were just a few of the operators that are available to you.

Evaluation Order

If you had expressions like 3+2*4, should the addition or the multiplication be done first? High school math tells you that multiplication has to be done first. This says the multiplication operator has the higher priority than the addition operator.

Changing the Order of Evaluation

To make an expression more readable, you can use parentheses. For example, 4+(2*3) is definitely easier to understand than 4+2*3, which requires knowing the operator precedence. As with anything else, the parentheses should be reasonable and shouldn't be redundant, such as (4+(2*3)).

There's another advantage to using parentheses. It helps you change the order of evaluation. For example, if you'd like addition to be calculated before multiplication is evaluated in an expression, then write something along the lines of (2+3)*6.

Associativity

Operators are most often associated from left to right, just like you read. This means the operator with the same precedence is evaluated in a left to right manner. For example, 1+2+3 is evaluated as (1+2) +3.

Expressions

Save the following example as expressions.py.

length = 7

width = 8

```python
area = length*width

print ('Area is',area)

print ('Perimeter is', 2 * (length + width))
```

Output:

```
$ Python expression.py

Area is 56

Perimeter is 30
```

The length and the width of the rectangle are stored in variables of the same name. You use them to calculate the area and the perimeter of the rectangle using expressions. You store the result of the expression length times width in the variable 'area' and then print it using the 'print' function. For the second example, you directly use the value of the expression 2 * (length + width) in the print function.

In addition, notice how Python pretty-prints your output. Even though you have not specified the space between 'Area is' and the variable area, the program will put it in for you so that you get a fresh, pleasant output and the program is a lot more readable that way.

Chapter Four

Control Flow

The programs you've seen so far have had a sequence of statements that are executed by Python in the top to bottom order. What if you wanted to change the flow of how the program worked? For example, maybe you'd like to make a program that would take some decisions and do something different depending on the different situation, such as printing 'Morning' or 'Evening' depending on the time of day.

You can achieve this utilizing control flow statements. Three statements in Python exist. These are *if, for,* and *while.*

The If Statement

This statement is used to check a condition. If the condition is true, then the program runs a block statements known as the if-block, else the program processes additional block of statements known as the else-block. Using the else clause is optional.

Save this example as if.py.

```
number = 27

guess = int(input('Enter a number: '))

If guess == number:

    #new block begins here

    print('You got it!')

    print('(but you don't win a prize.)')

    #new block ends

elif guess < number:

    #second block

    print('No, the number is greater')

else:

    print('No, it's less')

    #You must have guessed > number to get here
```

```
print('Done')

#this final statement will always be executed,

#after the if statement has been executed.
```

Output:

```
$ python if.py

Enter a number: 60

No, it's less

Done
```

```
$ python if.py

Enter a number: 24

No, the number is greater

Done
```

```
$ python if.py

Enter a number: 27

You got it!

(but you don't win a prize.)

Done
```

In the program, you take guesses from the user and check to see if it's the number that you have. You set the variable 'number' to any integer you'd prefer, such as 27. Then, you take the user's guess with the input() function. These are just reusable pieces of programs.

You supply a string to the built-in input function which then prints it to the screen and waits for the input from the user. Once something is entered, and the enter key is pressed, the input function returns what you entered as a string. Then this string is converted into an integer using the int, and it's stored in the variable guess. The int is a class, but all you have to know right now is that you're able to use it to convert a string to an integer.

Next, you compare the guess from the user with the number that's been chosen. If they're equal, then you print a success message. Notice the use of the indentation levels to tell the program which statements belong to which block. That's why indentation is so imperative.

Notice how your if statement has a colon at the end. When you do this, you indicate to the program that there is a block of statements that follows.

Then, you check if the guess is less than that number, and if it is, you inform the user that they guessed a little higher than the number.

The elif and the else statements have to have a colon at the end of the logical line follow by the block statements for them, with the proper indentations.

You can have another if statement inside the block of an if statement, which is known as a nested statement.

Remember that the elif and the else parts are both optional. A minimal valid one is:

if true:

```
print('Yes, it's true')
```

After the program has finished executing your whole if statement accompanied by the related elif and else clauses, it then moves on to the following statement in the block that has an if statement. In this case, it's the main one, and the next statement is the print('done') statement. After that, the program sees the end of the program and just finishes up.

The While Statement

The while statement lets you repeatedly execute a block of statements as long as the condition is true. A while statement is an example of what's known as a looping statement. They can have an optional else clause.

For example, save this program as while.py.

```python
number = 27

running = True

while running:

    guess = int(input("Put in a number: "))

    if guess == number:

        print('You got it.')

        running = False

    elif guess < number:

        print('No, it's higher.')
```

```python
    else:

        print('No, it's lower.')

    print('The while loop's finished.')

    print('Done')
```

In this program, you're still playing a guessing game, but the advantage is the user is able to keep guessing until they guess the right number, there's no need to repeatedly run the program for every guess as was done in the previous section. This demonstrates the use of the while statement.

You move the input and the if statements to the inside of your while loop and set the variable running to True before your loop. First, the while statement checks if the variable 'running' is equal to True and executes the while block if it is. Next, the if statement is evaluated and the corresponding true or false block is executed. The program then goes back to the while statement and checks the running variable again. This continues until the running variable contains the False value at which time the statement immediately following the while block will be executed.

The true and false are known as Boolean types and you can consider them equivalent to 1 and 0.

The For Loop

The for...in statement is another looping statement that iterates over a sequence of objects. What you need to know about sequencing as a beginner is that a sequence is an ordered collection of objects.

As an example, save this document as for.py:

```
for i in range (1,5):

        print(i)

print('the for loop is over')
```

Your output will be:

```
$ python for.py
```

2

3

4

The for loop is over

In this program your printing a sequence of numbers. You create this sequence using the built-in range function. What you're doing here is supplying it with two numbers and range returns a set of numbers beginning with the first number and up to the second one. For example, range(1,5) will give the sequence 1, 2, 3, 4. By default, the range proceeds with a step count of one. If you give a third number, now that turns into the step count, so range(1,5,3) gives (1, 4). Remember, it extends up to the second number, so it doesn't include the second number. Note that the range() creates only one number at a time, if you'd like to use the full list of numbers, call list() on the range(), such as list(range(5)) results in (1, 2, 3, 4).

The loop will then iterate over this range, for i in the range(1,5) it's equal to for i in (1,2,3,4), which is like assigning each object in the sequence to i one at a time, and then completing the block of statements for every value of i. In this instance, you just print the value of the block statement.

The Break Statement

This statement is utilized to break past a loop statement or stop the running of a looping statement, although the condition hasn't become false or the sequence of items hasn't been completely repeated over.

Something important to remember is that if you break out of the for or while loop, any corresponding blocks are not executed.

For example, save this document as break.py:

while True:

```
user_input=input('put something here:')

if user_input == 'quit':

    break

    print('the length of the input
is',len(user_input))

print('Done')
```

The output will be:

$ python break.py

Put something here: programming is amazing

The length of the input is 22

Put something here: when you're having fun

Length of the string is 22

Put something here: quit

Done

In this program, you are repeatedly taking the user's input and printing the length of the input every time. In addition, you're providing a special condition to stop the program by checking to see if the user has typed in 'quit.' You stop the program by breaking out of the loop and then reaching the end of the program.

The length of the input string is found using the built-in len function.

Remember, the break statement is able to be used with the for loop, too.

The Continue Statement

The continue statement is used to tell the program to skip the remaining statements in the loop block and to go on to the following repetition of the loop.

For example, save this document as continue.py:

```
while true:

    user_input = input ('put something here:')

    if user_input == 'quit':

        break

    if len(user_input) < 3:

        print('Nope, too small')
```

```python
        continue

    print('Input is of the right length)
```

The output would be:

```
$ python continue.py

Put something here: a

Nope, too small

Enter something: 13

Nope, too small

Enter something rtc

Input is of the right length

Enter something: quit
```

With this program, you accept input from the user, but you process the input string only if it's at least three characters long. So, you use the built-in len function to get the length, and if it's less than three, you skip the rest of the statements in the block by using your continue statement. The rest of the statements in the loop will be executed if you don't use the continue statement.

Chapter Five

Functions

Functions are a reusable piece of the program. They let you assign a designation to a block of statements, letting you run that block utilizing the designation anywhere in the program and at an unlimited amount. This is known as calling your function. You've already used many built-in functions, such as the range and the len functions.

The function concept is the most imperative building block of programming, so let's explore a few aspects of functions in this chapter.

Functions are defined using your def keyword. After this keyword comes the identifier name for your function, followed by some parenthesis that can enclose names of variables, and the final part is a colon at the end of the line. Next follows your block statements that are part of the function. An example would be:

Save this file as examplefunc1.py:

```python
def say_hello():

        print('Hello world')

say_hello()

say_hello()
```

The output would be:

```
$ python examplefunc1.py
```

Hello world

Hello world

A function is defined by using the say_hello syntax as seen above. This function does not take any parameters, and so there are no variables that are declared in the parentheses. Parameters to a function are just input to the function so you're able to pass in different values to it and get back a result.

Notice that you can call the same function twice, which means, you don't need to write the same code a second time.

Function Parameters

A function is able to take parameters, which are the values you supply to the function so it can do something with those values. These are just like a variable, except the values of them are defined when you call the function and are already assigned values when it runs.

Parameters will be specified in the pair of parentheses in the function's definition, separated by a comma. When you call the function, you supply the values the same way.

Let's look at an example. Save this document as function_parameters.py:

```
def print_max(a,b):

    if a > b:

        print(a, 'is max')

    elif a == b:

        print(a, 'equals', b)

    else:

        print(b, 'is max')

print_max(3,4)

x = 3

y = 5

print_max(x,y)
```

Output:

```
$ python function_parameters.py
```

4 is max

5 is max

Here, you define a function known as print_max that uses two parameters, and these are a and b. You found out the greater number with a simple if...else statement and then print the larger number.

The first time that you use the function print_max, you are using the numbers as arguments. When you use it in the second block, you are calling the function with the variables as arguments. Print_max (x,y) makes the value of the argument x assigned to the parameter a, and the value of the argument y is assigned as the parameter b. The print_max function works in the same way in both instances.

Local Variables

When you declare a variable inside a function definition, they're not related to the other variables with the same names that are used outside of the function; therefore, the variable names are local to the function. This is known as the scope of the variable. Every variable has the scope of the block they're declared in starting from the point of the definition of the name.

For example, save this document as function_local.py:

```
a=70

def func(a):

    print('a is', a)
```

```
a=3

    print('Changed local a to', a)

func(a)

print('a is still', a)
```

The output would be:

```
$ python function_local.py

a is 70

Changed local a to 3

a is still 70
```

The first time you print the value of the name x with the beginning line in the function's body, the program uses the value of the parameter that's declared in the main area, above the function definition.

Then, you assign the value three to x. The name x is local to the function. Therefore, when you change the value of x in the function, the x defined in the main block will remain the same.

With the last print statement, you display the value of x as defined in the main block, confirming that it's actually unaffected by the local assignment in the previously called function.

The Global Statement

If you'd like to assign a value to a name that's been defined at the top level of your program, then you have to tell the program that the name isn't local, but it's global. You can do this using the global statement. It's impossible to assign a value to a variable that's been defined outside the function without using a global statement.

You can use the values of these variables defined outside of the function. Yet, this isn't encouraged and ought to be evaded since it comes to be unclear to the person reading the program as to the location the variable's description is. Using the global statement makes it clear that the variable is defined in the outermost block.

As an example, save this document as global_function.py:

```
a=70

def func():

        global a

        print('a is', a)

        a=3

        print ('Switched global a to', a)

func()
```

```
print('The value of a is', a)
```

The output of this program would be:

```
$ python global_function.py
```

a is 70

Switched global a to 3

The value of a is 3

The global statement is used to declare x as a global variable; therefore, when you assign a value to x inside the function, this change is then reflected when you use the value x in your main block.

You can specify more than one of these types of variables using the same statement.

Default Argument Values

For some functions, you might want to make some parameters optional and use the default values in case the user doesn't want to provide a value for them. This is accomplished with the help of default argument values. You can stipulate default argument values meant for your parameters by attaching to the parameter name in the function definition the assignment operator (=) along with the default value.

Note the default argument value needs to be a constant.

As an example, save a document with this name default_function.py:

```python
def say (message, times=1):
    print(messages * times)

say('Hello')

say('world', 3)
```

The output would be as follows:

```
$ python default_function.py

Hello

worldworldworld
```

The function named 'say' is utilized to print a string as many times as you specify. If you don't supply it with a value, then it's just printed once. You can attain this by stipulating a default argument value of one to the parameter times.

Keyword Arguments

If you have functions that have more than one parameter, and you don't want to specify just a few of them, then you can give a value for these parameters by naming them. This is known as keyword arguments. You can use the name (keyword) rather than the position, which is what you've been using all along.

There are two advantages, one is using the function is easier because you don't need to worry about your argument orders. The second one is that you can give values to only those parameters that you want to, provided that the other parameters have a default argument value.

Save this document as an example, keyword_function.py:

```
def my_func(a,b=6, c=100):

    print('a is', a, 'and b is', b, 'and c is', c)

my_func(18)

my_func(27, c=100)

my_func(c=51, a=101)
```

The output of your program would be:

```
$ python keyword_function.py

a is 18 and b is 6 and c is 100

a is 27 and b is 6 and c is 100

a is 101 and b is 6 and c is 51.
```

The func function has one parameter without a default argument value, followed by two that do.

In the first use, func(3,7), the parameter a has a value of 3 while the parameter of b has a value of 7, and c has the default value of 92.

In the second one, func(25, c=92), the variable has a value of 25 because of the location of the argument. At that time, the parameter c has a value of 92 due to naming. The variable b has the default value of 7.

In the third one, func(c=50, a=100), you use the keyword arguments for the specified values. Notice that you are specifying the value for parameter c before the one for a even though it's defined before c in the function definition.

VarArgs Parameters

Sometimes, you might desire to define a function that could take any number of parameters, such as variable number of arguments, which can be achieved using stars.

Save this document as vararg_function.py:

```python
def total(start=5, *digits, **tokens):
    count=start

    for digit in digits:

        count+=digit

    for token in tokens:

        count+=tokens[token]

    return count

print(total(10,1,2,3, snakes=50 , lions=100))
```

The output would be:

$ python varargs_function.py

Declaring a starred parameter such as param, then all the positional arguments from this point until the end are collected as a tuple known as 'param'.

The Return Statement

This statement is utilized to return from a function or break out of the function. You can optionally return a value from the function, too. Let's look at an example.

Save this document as return_function.py:

```python
def maximum(x, z):

    if x>z:

        return x

    elif x==z:

        return 'these are equal'

    else:

        return z

print(maximum(2,3))
```

The output for the program will be:

$ python return_function.py

3

The maximum function will return the highest of the parameters, in this case, the numbers that were supplied to the function. It uses the simple if...else statement to figure out the greater value and then return that value.

Note that a return statement without the value equals a return of None. This is a special type in Python that represents nothingness. For example, it's used to indicate a variable doesn't have a value if it has a value of None.

Every function automatically has a return None statement at the end unless you've written a return statement.

DocStrings

This programming language has a nice feature known as documentation strings that are usually referred to as docstrings. These are an imperative tool that you need to make use of because they help you document the program better and make it easier for you to understand. You can get the docstring back from a program, even while it's running.

As an example, save this document as docstring_function.py:

def print_max(x,y):

    "'Prints the maximum of two numbers. The two values have to be integers.

```
    """

        x=int(x)

        y=int(y)

if x>y:

        print(x, 'is greater')

else:

        print(y, 'is greater')

print_max(3,5)

print(print_max.__doc__)
```

The output for the program would be:

$ python docstring_function.py

5 is greater

Prints the maximum of two numbers. The two values must be integers.

A string on the first logical line of the function is the docstring for it. Note that these also apply to classes and modules.

The convention that's used for a docstring is a multi-line string where the first line has a capital letter and ends with a dot. Then the second one is blank, followed by any detailed explanations beginning from the third line. You're advised to follow this convention for all docstrings for all non-trivial functions.

You can access the docstring of the print_max function with the __doc__ attribute of the function.

Chapter Six

Modules

You've observed how you can recycle code in the program by describing functions just the once. What if you'd like to recycle a number of functions in additional programs you create? Modules are the answer.

There are many methods of writing modules, but the easiest way is to make a file with the .py extension that has functions and variables in it.

Another method is to make the modules in the native language in which the interpreter is written. For example, you can make modules in the c programming language, and when it's compiled, they are used from the python code when using the standard python interpreter.

A module is able to be imported by another program to make use of the functionality. This is how you a can use python standard library, too. First, let's look at how to use the standard library modules.

Let's take a look at an example. Name the following file using_module_sys.py:

```
import sys

print('Arguments for the command line are:')
```

```
for a in sys.argv:

    print(a)

print('\n\nThePythonPath is', sys.path, '\n')
```

The output for this will be:

```
$ python using_module_sys.py we are arguments
```

Arguments for the command line are:

using_module_sys.py

we

are

arguments

The Python Path is['\tmp\py',

'/Library/Python/2.7/site-packages',

'/usr/local/lib/python2.7/site-packages']

First, you import the system module using the import statement. This translates to telling python that you want to use this module. The system module has functionality related to the python interpreter and the environment or the system.

When python uses the import system statement, it looks for the system module. It's one of the built-in modules, and so python knows where it can find it.

If it wasn't a compiled module, then the interpreter would search for it in the directories listed in its sys.path variable. If it's found, then the statements in the body of that module are run and it's made available for you to use. Note that the initialization is done only the first time you import the module.

The argv variable in the system module is utilized using the dotted notation. It indicates this name is part of the system module. Another advantage of this is that the name doesn't clash with any argv variables used in the program.

The sys.argv variable is a list of strings.

If you're using an IDE to use your programs, look for a way you can specify command line arguments to the program in the menus.

Here, when you execute the module_using_sys.py, you run the module with the python command and the other things that come next are arguments passed on to your program. The program stores this command line argument in the sys.argv variable for you to use.

Remember that the name of the script running is the first argument in the sys.argv list.

The sys.path has the list of directory names where modules are imported. Observe the first string in the sys.path is empty, which indicates the current directory is part of the sys.path which is the identical to the pythonpath environment variable. This translates to you being able to directly import modules that are located in the directory. Otherwise, you have to put the module in one of the directories that's listed in the sys.path.

Byte-compiled .pyc files

Importing a module is a costly affair when it comes to programming, so python does a few tricks to make it quicker. One way you can do this is by making a byte-compiled file with the extension .pyc, which is an intermediate form that the programming language is able to transform the program into. This .pyc file is a benefit when you import it the next time from another program. It'll be a lot faster since a portion of the processing that's required when importing a module is already completed. Also, these files are independent of platforms.

The from...import statement

If you'd like to directly import your argv variable into the program, now you can utilize the from sys import argv statement.

You should avoid using this in general because the program will avoid name clashes and it'll be more readable.

A module's __name__

Every module has one and statements in modules can be found out by the name of their module. This is good for the purpose of figuring out whether or not the module is being run standalone or it's imported. As aforementioned, when a module is imported for the first time, the code it has is executed. You can use this to make the module behave in a different way depending on whether it's being used by itself or it is being imported from another module. This is able to be achieved by using the __name__ attribute.

Save this as using_module_name.py:

```
if __name__ == '__main__':

        print('This is a program that's running by itself')

else:

        print('I'm being imported')
```

The output for these will be:

```
$ python using_module_name.py
```

This is a program that's running by itself

```
$ python

>>>import using_module_name

I'm being imported

>>>
```

Every python module has the name defined.

Making Your Own Modules

Making your own modules is easy. You've actually been doing it throughout this book. That's because every python program is actually a module. You just have to be sure it's a .py extension.

The Dir Function

You can use a built-in dir function to list the identifiers your object defines. For example, for the module, the identifiers are the functions, classes, and the variables defined in the module.

When you supply the module name to the dir() function, it gives back the list of the names defined in that module. When no argument is applied, then it returns the list of names that are defined in the current module.

As an example:

$ python

```
>>>import sys
```

```
>>>dir(sys)
['__displayhook__',' __doc__',
'argv', 'builtin_module_names',
'version', 'version_info']
```

You see the usage of dir on the imported sys module. You can see the list of attributes it has. This function works on any object, so run dir(str)for the attributes of the str(string) class.

Packages

You've most likely begun noticing the hierarchy of organizing a program. Variables almost always go in functions. Functions and global variables go inside the modules. What if you wanted to organize the modules? That's where packages come into play.

Packages are just the folders of modules with a special __init__.py file that tells python this folder is special because it has modules.

Let's say you'd like to make a package known as 'earth' with sub packages 'North America', 'Southeast Asia', and these sub packages turned into modules such as 'India', 'United States', etc.

This is how you'd structure those folders:

-<a folder that's present in the sys.path>/

   - earth/

      - __init__.py

      -north america/

         -__init__.py

         -united states/

         -__init__.py

         -foo.py

      -southeast asia/

```
-__init__.py

-India/

    -__init__.py

    -bar.py
```

This is how you'd structure them.

Chapter Seven

Data Structures

Data structures are what they sound like; they are structures that hold some data together. They're used to store a collection of related data to make life easier. There are four built-in ones to python, known as list, tuple, dictionary, and set. Let's look at how you can use all of them to make programming a little easier.

List

Lists are data structures that hold an orderly group of items. You can store a series of things in your list. This is easy to imagine if you'd think of a shopping list where you have a list of things you want to purchase, except you probably have them on a separate line in the shopping list, where in python you'd put commas between them.

The list of items should be put in a set of square brackets so the program understands you're specifying a list. Once you've made the list, you can add, remove, and search for things on it. Since you can add and remove items, you can say that a list is a mutable data type, meaning it can be altered.

Let's look at an example. Save this file as using_ds_list.py:

```
#This is a shopping list

shopping_list = ['peaches', 'carrots', 'mangoes', 'bananas']


print("I've got", len(shopping_list), 'items to buy.')


print('These are:')

for item in shopping_list:

        print(item)


print('\nI also have to purchase rice.')

shopping_list.append('rice')
```

```python
print('My shopping list now has', shopping_list)


print('I will sort this list now')

shopping_list.sort()

print('Sorted shopping list is', shopping_list)


print("The first item I'm going to buy is",
shopping_list[0])

olditem = shopping_list[0]

del shopping_list[0]

print('I purchased the', olditem)

print('My shopping list is', shopping_list)
```

The output for this program would be:

```
$ python using_ds_list.py
```

I've got 4 items to buy.

These are:

peaches

carrots

mangoes

bananas

I also have to purchase rice.

My shopping list now has ['peaches', 'carrots', 'mangoes', 'bananas', 'rice']

I will sort this list now

Sorted shopping list is ['bananas', 'carrots', 'mangoes', 'peaches', 'rice']

The first item I'm going to buy is bananas

I purchased the bananas

My shopping list is ['carrots', 'mangoes', 'peaches', 'rice']

The variable shopping_list is the shopping list for someone who's going to the grocery store. In shopping_list, you only store strings of the names of the things to purchase, but you could add any kind of object to a list including other lists and numbers.

You've also used the for..in loop to go through the items of the list. By now, you've probably realized this is also a sequence.

Next, you add an item to the list using the append method of the list object. You then check that the item was added to the list by printing the contents of it by passing to the print function that prints it for you.

Then, you sort your list by using the sort method. It's imperative to understand this method affects the list and doesn't return a modified list. This is different from the way strings operate. This is what it means by saying that a list is mutable and that a string is immutable.

Next, when you finish purchasing an item at the grocery store, you want to remove it from your list. You can achieve this by using the del statement. There, you mention which item of the list you'd like to remove and the del statement will remove it for you. You specify that you want to remove the first item from the list and you use the del shopping_list[0].

Tuple

These are used to hold together many objects at once. Think of them as a list, but without the extensive functionality you have from a list. One major feature of these is that they are immutable like the strings, which means you can't modify them.

These are defined by stipulating things separated with a comma in an elective pair of parentheses.

They're used in cases where a statement or a user-defined function can safely assume the collection of values used isn't going to change.

As an example, name this document using_ds_tuple.py:

```
zoological_park = ('elephant', 'snake', 'buffalo')

print('The number of animals in the zoological_park
is', len(zoological_park))


new_zoological_park = 'camel', 'monkey',
zoological_park

print('The number of cages in the new
zoological_park is', len(new_zoological_park))

print('All animals in the new zoological_park are',
new_zoological_park)

print('Animals that were brought from the old
zoological_park are', new_zoological_park[2])
```

print('The last animal brought from the old zoological_park is', new_zoological_park[2][2])

print('The number of animals in the new zoological_park is',

len(new_zoological_park)-1+len(new_zoological_park[2]))

The output for this program will be:

$ python ds_using_tuple.py

The number of animals in the zoological_park is 3

The numbers of cages in the new zoological_park is 3

All animals in the new zoological_park are ('camel', 'monkey', ('elephant', 'snake', 'buffalo'))

Animals that were brought from the old zoological_park are ('elephant', 'snake', 'buffalo)

The last animal brought from the old zoological_park is buffalo

The number of animals in the new zoological_park is 5

The variable zoo is referring to a tuple of items. You can see the len function is able to be used to get the length of the tuple. This indicates a tuple is a sequence, too.

You're now shifting these animals to the new zoo because the old zoo is closed. Therefore, the new_zoo tuple has some animals that are already there along with some ones that were brought over from the old zoo. Note that the tuple doesn't lose its identity.

You can access the items in the tuple by specifying its position in a pair of square brackets just like you did for the list. This is known as an indexing operator. You access the third one in the new_zoo by specifying new_zoo[2] and you access the third item in the third item in the new_zoo tuple by specifying new_zoo[2][2]. This is simple once you've understood the idiom.

Tuples with Zero or One Items

Empty tuples are created by an empty pair of parentheses such as myempty=(). Yet, a tuple with a single item isn't so simple. You have to specify it with a comma following the first item so that the program is able to differentiate between the tuple and a pair of parentheses surrounding the object in the expression.

Dictionary

Dictionaries are like address books where you're able to find the address or the contact details of the person by knowing their name, such as keys(name) with values(details). Note that the key has to be unique just like you can't find out the right information if you have two people with exactly the same names.

Take note that you're able to use only immutable objects, such as strings, for the keys of the dictionary, but you could use either mutable or immutable objects for the values of your dictionary. This basically says that you should use only simple objects for your keys.

Values and pairs of keys are specified in a dictionary by using the notation d = {key1: value1, key2: value2}. Notice the key-value pairs are separated by a colon and the pairs are separated by commas, and it's all placed in curly brackets.

Remember the key-value pairs in your dictionary are not ordered in any way. If you want a certain order, then you'll need to sort them before you use it.

The dictionaries you'll be using are instances or objects of the dict class.

For example, save this code as using_ds_dict.py:

```python
# 'ab' is short for address book


ab = {

        'Python': 'Python@swaroopch.com',

        'Larry': 'larry@example.com',

        'Matsumoto': 'matsumoto@example.com',

        'Spam': 'spam@example.com'

}


print("Python's address is", ab['Python'])
```

```python
# to delete a key-value pair

del ab['Spam']


print('\nThe address book has {} contacts in it
\n'.format(len(ab)))


for name, address in ab.items():

    print('contact {} at {}'.format(name, address))


#to add a key-value pair

ab['Someone'] = 'someone@somethin.com'


if 'Someone' in ab:
```

```
print("\nSomeone's address is",
```
ab['Someone'])

The output for this program would be:

$ python using_ds_dict.py

Python's address is Python@swaroopch.com

The address book has 3 contacts in it

contact Matsumoto at matsumoto@example.com

contact Python at Python@swaroopch.com

contact Larry at larry@example.com

Someone's address is *someone@somethin.com*

You've created the dictionary ab with the notation that was already discussed. Then you access the key-value sets by stipulating the key that's utilizing the indexing operator. You can see the simple syntax.

You can get rid of key-value pairs with the del statement by just specifying the dictionary and the indexing operator for it to be deleted and pass it to the del statement. There isn't any need to know the value that corresponds to the key for this statement.

Next, you access every key-value pair of the dictionary with the items method of the dictionary that returns a list of tuples where every tuple has a pair of items, the key followed by the value. You then retrieve it and assign it to the variables name and address that corresponds for every pair using the for..in loop and then print them in the for-block.

You can add new key-value pairs just by using the index operator to access the key and assign it a value, as you did for Someone's example in the aforementioned program.

You can check if a key-value pair exists with the in operator.

Sequence

Tuples, lists, and strings are all examples of sequences, but what are they and what is special about them?

The major features are membership tests and indexing operators, which let you fetch a certain item in the sequence directly.

The three types of sequences that are mentioned above also have the slicing operator that lets them retrieve a piece of the sequence.

For example, save this document as seq_ds.py:

```python
shopping_list = ['mango', 'carrot', 'banana']

name= 'Python'



# indexing or 'subscription' operation #

print('Item 0 is', shopping_list[0])

print('Item 1 is', shopping_list[1])

print('Item 2 is', shopping_list[2])



# how to slice on a list #

print('Item 0 to 2 is', shopping_list[0:2])
```

The output of this program would be:

```
$ python seq_ds.py
```

Item 0 is mango

Item 1 is carrot

Item 2 is banana

Item 0 to 2 is ['mango', 'carrot']

First, you can see how to use indexes to get the individuals items of the sequence. This is referred to as a subscription operation. Whenever you specify the number of a sequence in the square brackets as it's shown above, the program will get you the item that corresponds to that position in the sequence. Remember, the program begins counting numbers from zero; therefore, shopping_list[0] refers to the first item and shopping_list[2] refers to the third item on the list.

The index may also have a negative number where the position is calculated from the end of the sequence. Therefore, shopping_list[-1] would refer to the last item in the sequence and shopping_list[-2] would refer to the second to last item on the list.

The slicing operation is utilized by specifying the name of the sequence followed by the optional pair of numbers separated by a colon in the square brackets. Note that this is similar to the indexing operation you've been using until now. Remember, the numbers are optional, but your colon isn't.

The first number that comes before the colon in the slicing operation is referring to the position from where the slice begins and the second number indicates where the slice is going to stop. If the first number isn't specified, the program will begin at the beginning of the sequence. If the second number isn't put in, then the program will stop at the end of the sequence. Take note that the slice returned begins at the start position and ends just before the end position.

You can also do slicing with a negative position. Negative numbers are utilized for positions from the end of the sequence. For example, shopping_list[:-1] returns a slice of the sequence that excludes the last item of the sequence but still have everything else.

Set

These are unordered collections of objects. They are used when the existence of an object in a collection is more imperative than the order or how many times it happens.

Using sets, you can test for membership, whether it's a subset of another set, find the intersection between two sets, and so on and so forth.

References

When you make an object and assign it to a variable, the variable only refers to the object and doesn't actually represent it. The variable name is pointing to that part of the computer's memory where the object has been stored. This is known as binding the name to the object.

Usually, you don't have to be worried about this, but there's a subtle effect due to references that you should be aware of.

As an example, save this document as reference_ds.py:

```python
print('Easy Assignment')

shopping_list = ['peaches', 'apples', 'carrots', 'bananas']

#mylist is another name that's pointing to the same object.

mylist = shopping_list



#I've bought the first item, so I'm removing it from the list

del shopping_list[0]



print('shopping_list is', shopping_list)

print('mylist is', mylist)
```

#Take note that both of them print and they're the same list without the peaches, confirming they're pointing to the same object

print('copy by making a full slice')

#make a copy with a full slice

mylist = shopping_list[:]

#remove the first item

del mylist[0]

print('shopping_list is', shopping_list)

print('mylist is', mylist)

notice that the two lists are now different

This will be the output for the program:

```
$ python reference_ds.py

Easy Assignment

shopping_list is ['apples', 'carrots', 'bananas']

mylist is ['apples', 'carrots', 'bananas']

copy by making a full slice

shopping_list is ['apples', 'carrots', 'bananas']

mylist is ['carrots', 'bananas']
```

Remember, if you want to make a copy of a list or such types of sequences or complex objects, then you need to use the slicing operation to make a copy. If you just assign the variable name to another name, then both of them refer to the same object, and this might mean trouble if you're not careful.

Chapter Eight

Input and Output

There are circumstances where your program needs to cooperate with users. For example, you'll want to receive feedback from the user and then print results back to them. You can do this by using the input() function and print function. For output, you can also use a few methods of the str class. For example, you can use the rjust method in order to obtain a string that's right justified to a specified width.

Another common type of input and output is files. The ability to make, read, and write a file is essential to numerous programs, and we'll explore that in this chapter.

As an example of input from the user, save this file as input_io.py:

```python
def reverse(input):

        return input[::-1]


def is_palindrome(input):

    return input == reverse(input)


anything = input("Enter text:")
```

```python
if is_palindrome(anything):

    print("Yes, it's a palindrome")

else:

    print("No, it's not a palindrome")
```

The output for this program would be:

```
$ python3 input_io.py

Enter text: sir

No it's not a palindrome


$ python3 input_io.py

Enter text: madam

Yes, it's a palindrome
```

You're using the slicing feature to reverse the text. You've already seen how you can make slices with sequences using the seq[a:b] code beginning from position a to position b. You can also give it a third argument that determines the step by which the slicing occurs. The default step is one because of which returns a continuous part of text. Giving a negative step, such as negative one, will return the text in reverse.

The input() function takes a string as an argument and displays it to the viewer. Then it waits for them to type something and press the enter key. Once the user has entered text and pressed the return key, the input() function then returns that text the user has entered.

You're taking that text and reversing it. If the original text and reverse text match, then the text is a palindrome.

Files

You're able to open and use files for writing or reading by making an object of the file class and using it's read, readline or write methods correctly to read from or write to that file. The ability to read or write to your files depends on the mode you've specified for the file opening. Then finally, when you're finished with the file, you'll call the close method to tell the program that you're done using the file.

For an example, save the following file as using_io_file.py:

```
rhyme='''\

Programming's fun

When the work's done

If you want to make your work fun:

    Use Python!'''



f = open('rhyme.txt', 'w')



f.write(rhyme)

#close the file

f.close()
```

```python
f = open('rhyme.txt')

while True:

        line = f.readline()

        if len(line) == 0:

                break

        #the 'line' already has a new line at the end of
each line, since it's reading from a file

        print(line, end='')

f.close()
```

The output for this program would be:

$ python3 using_io_file.py

Programming's fun

When the work's done

If you want to make your work fun

Use python!

First, you're opening a file by using the built-in open function and specifying the name of it and the mode in which you want to open it. The mode is read as ('r'), append mode ('a'), or write mode ('w'). You can also stipulate whether you're reading, appending, or writing in binary mode ('b') or text mode ('t'). There are many more that are available that you will learn as you keep using python.

In the previous example, you first open the file in write text mode and utilize the write technique of the file object to write to the file and then you close it.

Next, you open the same file again for reading. You don't need to specify a mode because 'read text file' is the default one. You read in every line of the file using the readline method in the loop. This technique returns a whole line with the newline character at the conclusion of the line. When the vacant string is returned, it means you have reached the end of the file and you break out of the loop.

In the end, you finally close the file.

Now, check the contents of the rhyme.txt file to confirm the program has written and read from that file.

Pickle

Python provides a standard module known as pickle which you can use to store any plain python object in a file and then retrieve it later. This is known as storing the object persistently.

Save this example program as the file pickle_io.py:

```
import pickle
```

```
#the name of the file where you will store the object

shoplistfile = 'shopping_list.data'

# the list of things to purchase

shopping_list = ['mango', 'apples', 'carrot']
```

```python
# write to the file

f = open(shoplistfile, 'wb')

#dump the object to the file

pickle.dump(shopping_list, f)

f.close()



#destroy the shopping_list variable

del shopping_list



#read back from the storage

f = open(shoplistfile, 'rb')

# load the object from the file

storedlist = pickle.load(f)
```

print(storedlist)

The output for this program would be:

$ python pickle_io.py

['mango', 'apple', 'carrot']

How It Works

To store an object in a file, you have to first open the file to write binary modeNext, call the dump function of the pickle module; known as pickling.

Next, you retrieve the object using the load function of the pickle module which returns your object. This process is known as unpickling.

Unicode

So far, when you've been writing and using strings, or reading and writing to a file, you've used simple English characters.

When you read or write to a file or when you talk to their computers through the internet, you have to convert your Unicode strings into a format that's able to be sent and received, and that format is known as UTF-8. You can read and write in that format with a simple keyword argument to your standard open function:

```
# encoading=utf-8
```

```
import io


f = io.open("xyz.txt", "wt", encoding="utf-8")

f.write(u"Imagine a non-English language here,
Представьте себе, не английский язык здесь")

f.close()


text = io.open("xyz.txt", encoding="utf-8").read()

print(text)
```

You can ignore the import statement for the moment. Whenever you write a program that uses Unicode literals like you've used above, you have to be sure the program is told that your program uses UTF-8, and you have to put # encoding=utf-8 comment at the program top.

You can use io.open and provide the "encoding" and "decoding" argument to let the language know that you're using Unicode.

Conclusion

Congratulations on completing the Python basic apprenticeship and successfully navigating your first Python project! In this book, I hope I have managed to give you all the information you need to feel confident in your ability to move forward and try some more difficult Python projects. Good luck!

A message from the author,

Steve Gold

To show my appreciation for your support, Id like to offer you a couple of exclusive free gifts:

FREE BONUS!

As a free bonus, I've included a preview of one of my other best-selling books directly after this section. Enjoy!

ALSO...

Be sure to check out my other books. Scroll to the back of this book for a list of other books written by me, along with download links.

Finally, if you enjoyed this book, **please** take the time to post a review on Amazon. It will only take a couple of minutes and I'd be extremely grateful for your support.

Thank you again for your support.

Steve Gold

FREE BONUS!: Preview Of "Arduino: Getting Started With Arduino: The Ultimate Beginner's Guide"!

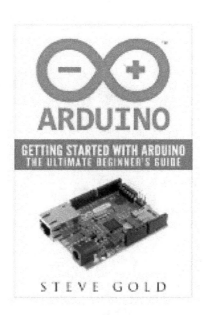

If you enjoyed this book, I have a little bonus for you;

a preview of one of my other books "**Arduino:**

Getting Started With Arduino: The Ultimate

Beginner's Guide". In this book, I'll show you just how incredible Arduino is, as well as how to complete your first Arduino project. Enjoy the free sample, and feel free to click on the purchase link below if you would like to learn more!

Introduction

If are you fascinated by the simplest of technology, and often wonder about the inner workings of the electronic devices that are ubiquitous in our daily lives, you are likely to find joy in experimenting and tinkering with Arduino.

At the core of everything that comes to life at a flick of a switch – the Christmas tree lights that blink in multiple colors, the apps that open up on a touch screen device, and the microwave oven that heats up your food etc. – is a micro-controller, programmed to perform certain feats when activated. Arduino is an open-source platform that consists of a micro-controller and programming software. Unlike most platforms, Arduino was geared towards non-electricians who want to get creative with electronics, while also being flexible enough to accommodate engineering experts. It is meant to be accessible, low cost and easy to learn, regardless of your previous knowledge in electronics and programming.

This guide will not make you an Arduino expert overnight – in fact, nothing can. What you will learn from this book however are the fundamentals of this amazingly versatile platform, and you'll also have the opportunity to get a firsthand feel for what it can do. You will be guided through the key features of an Arduino circuit board, technical requirements to begin working, how to kick-start your first Arduino, important lingo you'll need to know in order to get by, and how to proceed further in order to keep building upon what you have learnt.

The information here is intended for the absolute beginner in electronics, circuitry and programming. If you have always wanted to learn how to build cool stuff with electronics yet are completely at loss as to how to get started, you now have all the information you'll need at your fingertips in order to make your entry into the exciting world of Arduino. The rest is up to you!

Chapter 1

Understanding Arduino

In 2005, the Ivrea Interaction Design Institute in Italy started a project of creating an open-source platform to be used for building various electronic projects, known as Arduino. Originally geared towards students with little to no background in electronics or computer programming, the platform eventually gained worldwide popularity due to its accessibility and beginner-friendly features.

Over the years since its inception, Arduino has garnered the attention and enthusiasm of hobbyists, artists, programmers, students and even hackers from all levels of experience. Being an open-source platform, it continues to grow with contributions from a diverse community of users that keep pushing the limits of its capabilities. In fact, Arduino has been the backbone behind thousands of projects and applications, from everyday objects to complex scientific equipment.

The Arduino platform consists of two components:

1. **The hardware** – A physical programmable circuit board, also known as the microcontroller. There are different types of Arduino boards (more on this in Chapter 2).

2. **The Software** – The Integrated Development Environment (IDE) that runs on the computer, used for writing and uploading programming codes to the physical board.

Why Go Arduino?

Practically anyone can use Arduino. Experts are sure to have fun with building projects and sharing ideas with other users at online communities. For those with no experience with circuits and micro-controller programming, the platform is excellent for learning and experimenting. However, it is recommended that before exploring the wonders of Arduino, you should at least have a firm understanding of these fundamental concepts:

- The basics of electricity and circuitry

- Voltage, current, resistance and Ohm's law

- Polarity

- Integrated circuits (ICs)

- Digital logic

- Analog versus Digital

- Basic computer programming

What makes Arduino a favorite among amateurs and experts alike is that, compared to other platforms and systems, it simplifies the process of working with micro-controllers. For a start, loading new codes to the board can simply be done with a USB cable, unlike previous programmable circuit boards where a separate piece of hardware has to be used. It is also a plus point that Arduino boards are relatively inexpensive compared to other micro-controller platforms, with some pre-assembled modules costing less than $50. If those perks are not enough, here are some more reasons why Arduino is the platform to go for:

- **Cross-platform** – Arduino's IDE runs on Windows, Macintosh OSX, and Linux operating systems, whereas most micro-controller systems are only compatible with Windows.

- **Simple programming environment** – The Arduino IDE uses a simplified version of C++, making it easier for beginner to learn how to program, yet flexible enough for advance users to get creative and ambitious with.

- **Open source and extensible hardware** – Arduino board plans are published under a Creative Common license, allowing circuit designers to create their own version of the module, extending it and improving upon it.

- **Open source and extensible software** – The Arduino IDE is published as open source tools that experienced programmers can expand on, through C++ libraries. You can also learn the AVR-C programming language from Arduino, just as you can also add AVR-C code directly into Arduino programs.

- **Backed by a supportive community** – If you are absolutely new to the platform and don't know where to begin, there is a wealth of information to be found online due to the popularity of Arduino. You will never run out of resources to learn from, and you can even find pre-coded projects to work on right away (See Chapter 5 for Arduino resources).

What can Arduino do for You?

Arduino was designed with the creative and innovative in mind, regardless of experience level. Artists, designers, electricians, engineers, programmers and science enthusiasts can use it to create interactive objects and environments. Among the things Arduino can interact with include motors, speakers, LEDs, GPS units, cameras, TVs, smartphones and even the internet.

With Arduino, one can build low cost scientific instruments, do programming for robotics, build interactive prototypes of architectural designs and create installations for musical instruments to experiment with sound, build new video game hardware – and this is just the tip of the iceberg! So, whether your project entails building a robot, a heating blanket, a festive lighting display or a fortune-telling machine, Arduino can serve as a base for your electronic projects.

Click here to check out the rest of "Arduino: Getting Started With Arduino: The Ultimate Beginner's Guide" on Amazon.

Check Out My Other Books!

Elon Musk - The Biography Of A Modern Day Renaissance Man

Elon Musk - The Business & Life Lessons Of A Modern Day Renaissance Man

Warren Buffett - The Business And Life Lessons Of An Investment Genius, Magnate And Philanthropist

Steve Jobs - The Biography & Lessons Of The Mastermind Behind Apple

Management - Achieve Management Excellence & World Class Leadership Skills In 7 Simple Steps

Sales - Easily Sell Anything To Anyone & Achieve Sales Excellence In 7 Simple Steps

Arduino - Getting Started With Arduino: The Ultimate Beginner's Guide

(If the links do not work, for whatever reason, you can simply search for these titles on the Amazon to find them. All books available as ebooks or printed books)